To J.C.

HH

Heather Hill

Cover & Art BNelson

ISBN-13- 978-1978065253 ISBN-10-1978065256

Fowl Play
The Secret Life of Ducks

Brent Nelson

I like ducks.

I like to watch them
I like to feed them.
I like to read about them.

I've liked ducks
ever since I was a kid.

These are some of my favorite ducks.
Are any of them your favorite, too?

It is winter and the world is asleep.

So, ducks fly in looking for
each other's company to keep.

They gather on the water,

and in the snow on the shore.

Soon winter will be no more.

Spring will bring
warm weather to everything.

In the spring ducks
swim and play,

in the water
every day.

Ducks lay their eggs
in the sun.

Then watch over them,
every one.

When the eggs hatch,
the ducklings and their kin,

go down to the water
and go for a swim.

They like to swim
past the weeds.

Then they play
in the reeds.

Many different kinds of
ducks come and play.

They like to swim in
the sun every day.

Lots of ducks fly in for the summer.

Later, geese join them,
they're the latecomer.

They also like to swim and play,

before going on their way.

They walk along
the shore.

They get a drink,
then drink some more.

In the fall, they will fly south
before the winter snow.

They are making plans
right now to go.

Meanwhile, the ducks enjoy
the long summer days.

They run and play
in the sun's warm rays.

The ducks swim around the pond
looking for food to eat.

Some like small fish,
for others plants are a treat.

The ducks like to explore.
Some go it alone,

some go in groups,
others stay close to home.

As fall sets in, winter
will soon be here.

So, it's time to say good bye,
to the ducks for another year.

HH
Heather Hill